The Building Site

Dee Reid

Contents

Backhoe loader 2
Crane 6
Concrete mixer lorry ... 10
Architect 14

This is a backhoe loader.

It has a big bucket.

First, the bucket scoops up the earth.

Then, the shovel pushes the earth away.

This is a crane.

It has a long arm.

First, the crane lifts heavy blocks.

Then, the arm swings the blocks into place.

This is a concrete mixer lorry.

It pours concrete into the concrete pump.

First, the pump sucks up the concrete.

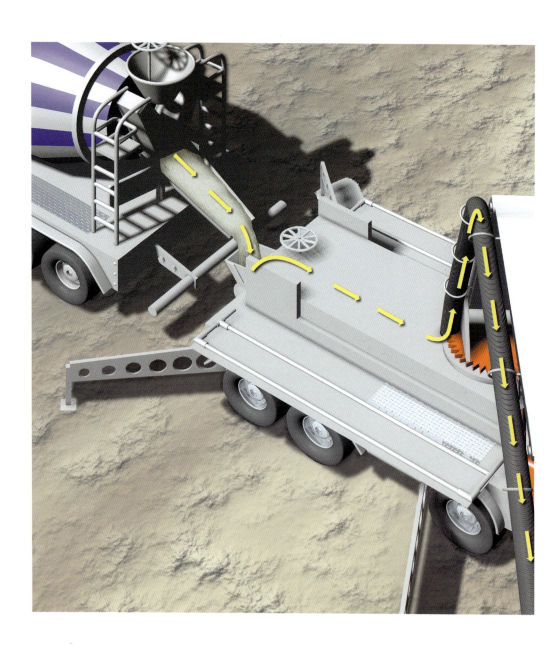

Then, the concrete is poured into the hole.

This is the architect.

She has designed the building.

Can you guess what is being built?